CW01647282

GREATEST POP STARS

VIP ACCESS!

Scan the QR code to
hear this story for

FREE!

Published in the UK by Sweet Cherry Publishing Limited, 2026
Unit 4u18, The Book Brothers Business Park, Tolwell Road,
Leicester LE4 1BR, United Kingdom

Sweet Cherry Publishing Limited
Unit 31, The Pottery, Bakers Point,
Pottery Road, Dún Laoghaire,
Dublin A96 EV18, Ireland

SWEET CHERRY and associated logos are trademarks and/or registered trademarks of Sweet Cherry Publishing Limited.

2 4 6 8 10 9 7 5 3 1

ISBN: 978-1-83689-116-1

Greatest Pop Stars:
Taylor Swift

© Sweet Cherry Publishing Limited, 2026

Text by Annabelle Coleman
Illustrations by Sophie Jones and Megan Mealing

All rights reserved. No part of this publication may be reproduced or utilised in any form or by any means, electronic or mechanical, including photocopying, recording, or using any information storage and retrieval system, without prior permission in writing from the publisher. No part of this publication may be used or reproduced in any manner for the purpose of training artificial intelligence technologies or systems.

The right of Annabelle Coleman to be identified as the author of this work has been asserted by them in accordance with the Copyright, Designs and Patents Act 1988.

This book is not authorised, licensed or approved by Taylor Swift. Any faults are the publisher's, who will be happy to rectify for future printings.

www.sweetcherrypublishing.com

Printed and bound in Turkey

MIX
Paper | Supporting responsible forestry
FSC® C221129

Sweet Cherry

TAYLOR SWIFT

THE UNOFFICIAL STORY

WRITTEN BY

ANNABELLE COLEMAN

CONTENTS

1

RISING STAR

In December 2024 at BC Place stadium in Vancouver, Canada, Taylor Swift was preparing for her final show on the Eras Tour. Over the course of almost two years, Taylor had performed 149 shows across 50 countries. The stage was set with dazzling lights and the crowd buzzed

with energy. Taylor changed from sparkly jackets to flowing gowns to glittery bodysuits. Her emotions shone through as she sang.

Taylor was a little teary-eyed, grateful for all the love from her fans and sad that this special chapter was ending. But she gave it her all, making the night unforgettable with every song she sang.

Taylor Alison Swift was born on the 13th of December 1989 and grew up on a Christmas tree farm with her parents, Scott and Andrea, and her little brother, Austin. Taylor's grandmother was an opera singer, and Taylor loved hearing her sing in church. Taylor decided she wanted to be a singer too. But it was country music she liked the best. She didn't just want to be a singer. She wanted to be a *country* singer.

Taylor loved country artists like The Chicks, Shania Twain and Patsy Cline, but her favourite was LeAnn Rimes. She wrote lots of fan letters to LeAnn and sent her drawings of them together. When Taylor was eight years old, she went to see LeAnn in concert and was lucky enough to meet her. She was holding a sign that said *I LOVE YOU LEANN!* And when LeAnn went to shake hands with her fans, Taylor asked, 'Did you get my letters?'

'I sure did, Taylor,' LeAnn replied. Taylor was beside herself with excitement at meeting one of her favourite singers! It made her even more determined to achieve her own dream.

Her parents supported her love for country music and took her to country festivals, fairs

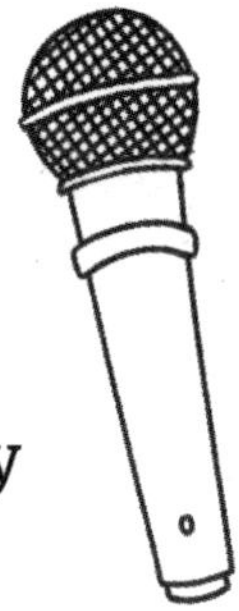

and karaoke competitions. A weekly singing contest that Taylor entered was run by legendary country singer Pat Garrett. Taylor took part every week from the age of ten.

'I'll keep entering until you let me win,' Taylor told Pat. Taylor was determined to prove herself, and she took every opportunity to improve her singing. But while she was having the best time performing, things weren't so perfect away from the stage.

While she was putting her all into her dream, she was lonely when she was at school. A lot of the other kids didn't understand Taylor's interest in country music and were mean to her. Taylor was hurt by their unkind words, but she didn't let that stop her. After learning that Faith Hill and Shania Twain, two country stars, started their careers in Nashville, Tennessee, she asked her parents to take her there too. But despite their support, she had to wait a little while before they could go because she was still so young.

In the meantime, Taylor made sure to have something

to show to music producers in Nashville when she did finally get there. All by herself, she recorded herself singing covers of her favourite songs and put them together on an album.

Eventually, when she was eleven years old, Taylor and her family went on a trip to Nashville. Her mother drove up and down the famous Music Row, where all the producers worked. While her family waited in the car, Taylor ran inside each studio with a copy of her album. But none of the producers called her to say they liked it. Taylor knew that if she really wanted to stand out, she was going to have to show everyone just how special she was.

2

FINDING HER VOICE

Taylor was disappointed after an unsuccessful start with the covers album, but she wasn't ready to quit. To get noticed she knew she had to be original, so she started writing her own songs. She learnt to play the guitar with the help of a family friend called Ronnie Cremer.

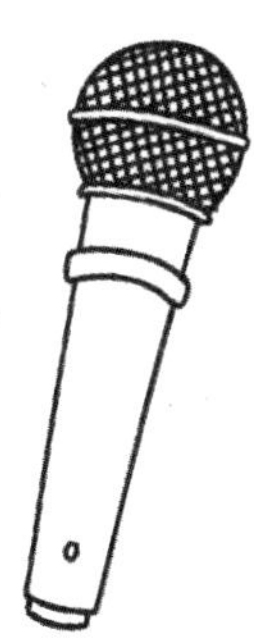

He was a computer repairman and, more importantly for Taylor, a local musician. Ronnie taught Taylor how to play her first guitar chords, which then helped her to write her first song. It was called 'Lucky You'. She wrote it when she was twelve years old, and it was about a little girl with a big heart and big dreams.

After penning that first song, Taylor didn't stop. She kept writing

and playing guitar, and got better and better. During that time she wrote a song called

'The Outside' about how hard school was. She wrote it after seeing how her classmates ignored her and kept her out of their conversations. Writing about her feelings allowed Taylor to let all of her emotions out. It helped her to understand what she was feeling and channel her negative emotions into something positive.

After two years of hard work on her music, Taylor returned to Nashville, ready to prove herself. Thanks to all the effort she had put in, she was successful this time!

At only thirteen, she signed a development deal with RCA Records. A development deal is when a record label helps an artist to develop their skills and take their first official steps into the industry. Now that Taylor's talent was being recognised, her family moved from Pennsylvania to Nashville so Taylor could really break into the country music industry.

Because she was so young, Taylor still had to go to school, but every Tuesday after class she worked with songwriters, including Liz Rose, an experienced,

professional writer. Together, they made songs inspired by Taylor's life and experiences.

Despite only being fourteen, Taylor worried that time was running out for her. Over the last year, RCA hadn't let her release her own music, even though she had written lots of promising songs. People in the industry were nervous about someone so young working in the cut-throat music business, so RCA wanted her to start out by singing other artists' songs instead of her own.

But that wasn't enough for Taylor. She soon decided that this wasn't working for her. One night, at the Bluebird Cafe in Nashville, she performed some of her own music. Little did she know that Scott Borchetta, the head of a record label, was in the audience. Scott was starting a brand-new company called Big Machine Records. After seeing Taylor perform, Scott signed her to Big Machine! Finally, she was on her way to becoming a professional country singer!

3

TAYLOR SWIFT

Taylor was really excited to be finally recording her first album. She worked with different songwriters including Liz Rose and a new producer called Nathan Chapman. She co-wrote eight songs and wrote three all by herself. Taylor was still new to the music industry and unknown outside of

Nashville. She had to work hard to prove that she was talented.

But she wasn't the only one with something to prove. Big Machine was a new company with no more than ten employees. If they wanted to be taken seriously, they had to make sure the music they put out was the best it could be. Everyone had to pitch in. Taylor, her mother and Nathan helped mail copies of the debut album to radio stations. While Taylor needed the help of Big Machine to make her dreams come true,

Big Machine also needed Taylor to make *theirs* a reality.

Introducing herself to the world, Taylor named her first album after herself. *Taylor Swift* was released in October 2006 and peaked at number five on the Billboard 200 chart. It was a huge success, staying in the charts for 157 weeks – the longest any album released in the 2000s had stayed in the charts. Not only that, but the album also became platinum certified, meaning it had sold over one million copies!

From the album, Taylor released five singles. These were 'Tim McGraw', 'Teardrops on My Guitar', 'Our Song', 'Picture to Burn' and 'Should've Said No'. Every single one made it onto the Billboard Hot Country Songs chart, with 'Our Song' and 'Should've Said No' reaching number one. She became the youngest female country singer to reach number one with a song she wrote herself!

It was an amazing result for her debut. The album was a hit with the public, but most of all with other teenage girls. Rather than singing about topics that were common in the country music genre, she wrote confessions based on her experiences in school.

The songs were about growing up, deciding who to be as a person and high school crushes, all written by a teenager. And fans couldn't help but speculate – who *were* the boys she was singing about?

The lead single, 'Tim McGraw', was about a relationship with a boy who was going to break up with her. By being so honest about

her love life and the different boys she had dated or had crushes on, Taylor attracted an audience who wanted to listen to the kind of music she made.

The album's success didn't end with the charts and audiences. Taylor won lots of awards, including Songwriter/Artist of the Year from the Nashville Songwriter Association, and the Academy of Country Music Awards Top New Female Vocalist. She even won Best New Artist at the 50th Annual Grammy Awards, one of the

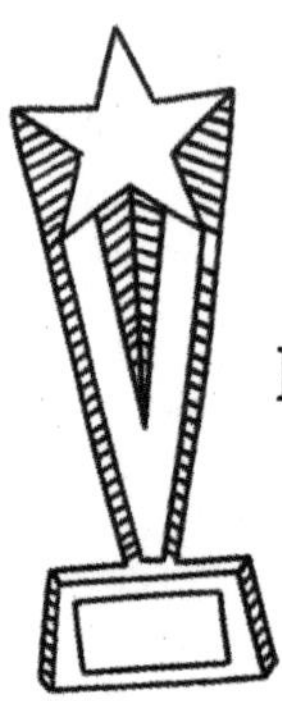

most prestigious awards in the music industry!

Taylor's career was finally taking off the way she had always dreamt. She had a string of successful songs in the charts and an album that was selling millions of copies. But little did she know, this was just the start for her, and soon she'd have new inspiration.

4

FEARLESS

With her music out in the world and being well received, Taylor was on to her next new experience as a rising artist: touring. To promote her debut album, she toured with country musician Brad Paisley between 2007 and 2008, and opened shows for other artists like Keith Urban and

Rascal Flatts. During these tours, she worked on her next album, called *Fearless*.

The album marked growth in Taylor as an artist. She started to move beyond traditional country sounds to country-pop fusion. *Fearless* was an intimate album about fairy-tale endings and true love, and it was more upbeat and less about her real life than her last album.

Fearless was released in November 2008 and was an even bigger success than *Taylor Swift*. It stayed at number one on the Billboard charts for eleven weeks and was the bestselling album in the USA in 2009. If *Taylor Swift* had established Taylor as a talented artist, then *Fearless* proved she was a budding legend.

Singles from the album included 'Love Story', 'White Horse', 'You Belong With Me', 'Fifteen' and the title track 'Fearless', all of which became fan favourites and huge successes. But it was 'Love Story', a reimagining of *Romeo and Juliet* that became a smash hit. It was a huge song in the USA and across the

globe, bringing her to the attention of audiences outside of the USA, such as in the UK and Australia.

Just as her first album had spoken to many teenage girls who might have shared Taylor's dreams and interests, *Fearless* became the go-to album for people who loved stories about romance and heartache.

But with all this success came a new level of attention for Taylor. Her career was going from strength to strength, and people started to recognise her name and style. She was starting to become a celebrity. Her first headline tour filled stadiums – something unheard of in the industry – and she was the bestselling artist of 2008 and 2009.

Her song 'White Horse' was featured in an episode of one of her favourite TV shows, *Grey's Anatomy*. She also wrote some songs for *Hannah Montana: The Movie* – and even had a small cameo part in the film!

She also wrote a song for romantic comedy *Valentines Day* and played a small role in the film.

While filming, Taylor grew close to her on-screen partner Taylor Lautner and the pair started a short-lasting relationship.

But there was another famous boyfriend who left a lasting impression on Taylor's legacy.

In 2008, while she was still working on *Fearless*, Taylor opened some shows for the musical group the Jonas Brothers. At the time, they were one of the biggest boy bands in the world. Taylor and Joe Jonas started dating but broke up shortly before *Fearless* came out.

However, this didn't stop Taylor writing songs about him. Just before the album was released, she added the song 'Forever & Always' which was about their breakup. Though their breakup upset Taylor, she didn't lose hope that one day she'd meet her own Prince Charming. 'Someday I'm gonna find somebody really, really, really great, who's right for me,' she said.

But little did anyone know that the defining moment of the era was still to come. At the 2009 MTV Music Video Awards, the music video for

'You Belong with Me' won the award for Best Female Video. Taylor had beaten famous pop icons like Lady Gaga, Katy Perry, Kelly Clarkson and even Beyoncé, one of the biggest pop singers in the world!

'Thank you so much!' said Taylor, accepting the award. 'I always dreamed about what it would be like to maybe win one of these someday but I never actually thought it would happen.' That night, Taylor had become the first country singer to win a VMA, but during her acceptance speech she was interrupted by the rapper Ye (previously called Kanye West). He took the mic from Taylor and talked about how Beyoncé's video for the song 'Single Ladies', also nominated for the award, was one of the best ever made.

No one could believe it, least of all Taylor. At first she had been excited to be on the same stage as Ye, but that changed very quickly once she realised what he was saying. One second she was accepting her award and the next, someone was suggesting she didn't deserve it.

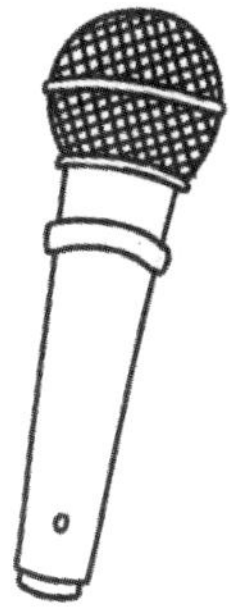

Thankfully, very few people agreed with Ye and a lot of people sided with Taylor, including President Obama. Later in the show, when Beyoncé won an award, she invited Taylor back on stage to finish her acceptance speech without being interrupted.

While it wasn't the best memory for Taylor, it was certainly something everyone remembered and talked about. If people didn't know who Taylor Swift was before, they did now.

5

SPEAK NOW

After the crazy success of *Fearless*, Taylor knew she had to follow it up with something even better. However, as her popularity rose, so did the criticism. At such a young age, a lot of people didn't believe she was capable of writing such good songs. So to prove them wrong, Taylor decided to try something new.

She started the writing process while on tour to promote *Fearless*, working on her new songs between shows. Normally she would write a bit and then take it to her co-writers who would help her finish it, but this time she decided to write all of the songs alone. While she did some songwriting with Nathan Chapman again, none of these were included in the final version of the album, making this new album the first one Taylor wrote all by herself.

A lot had changed in Taylor's life since her last album and her new music marked her transition into adulthood and fame. She was no longer writing about boys from high school but celebrities like her, and about her place in the world

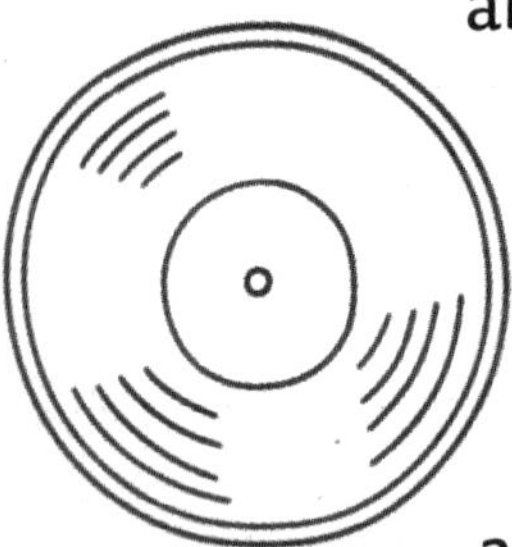

of music. She was now living alone for the first time, in a fancy apartment in Nashville. By this point, Taylor was an adult and an experienced artist in the industry, and her new album, *Speak Now,* reflected that. Instead of focusing on fairy-tale-inspired romances, it was centred on all the things she wished she had said to people who had hurt her, especially ex-boyfriends.

Another theme of the album was defending herself from criticism. Not only did people not believe Taylor was writing her own songs, but they also found fault with her singing skills. During the 2010 Grammy Awards, Taylor performed the song 'Rhiannon' with the legendary singer Stevie Nicks. While she had won four awards that night, her performance with Stevie wasn't well received, and people quickly began to say she wasn't a good singer. Understandably, Taylor was upset by this, so she wrote the song 'Mean' in response. It was a call back to her roots as a country artist and was about the harsh comments she had received throughout her career.

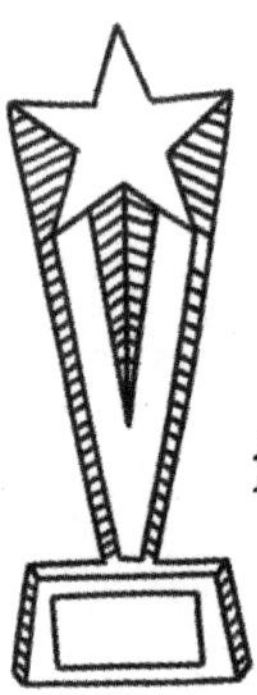

The track became an anti-bullying anthem, and at the 2012 Grammys it won awards for Best Country Song and Best Country Solo Performance, proving all her critics wrong. It wasn't the only song that was a response to things that had happened to Taylor in the industry. The incident with Ye at the 2009 VMAs was still at the forefront of her mind. But rather than criticising his actions, Taylor wrote 'Innocent' as a way of sympathising with Ye, and the song was about how people who do wrong things can make amends and learn from them. She dedicated the song to him, and the two struck up a friendship.

By including songs that were about personal topics in her album, Taylor wanted to show people she wasn't just a teenager with dreams anymore. She was a young woman trying to pave her way in a challenging industry. Her songs weren't about teenage romance anymore, but personal experiences that weren't necessarily relatable to her audience. But that didn't matter – people still wanted to hear what she had to sing about.

6

RED

While on tour for *Speak Now*, Taylor invited other famous singers to join her at different shows. The list included icons from lots of different music genres, like Justin Bieber, Selena Gomez, Nicki Minaj, Usher, B.o.B and Flo Rida.

During these performances, she

and the guest artist performed songs together. Working with these other artists was a great experience. It gave Taylor the opportunity to try out new genres and styles, and their work really influenced how she performed.

After the tour ended, Taylor felt inspired. She wanted to give herself a new challenge and leave her comfort zone. And how better to do just that than with a new album! She knew that for the next album she wanted a total change from *Speak Now*.

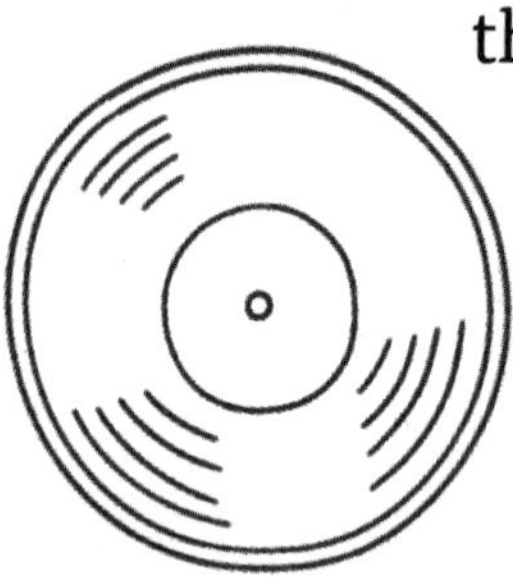

Just like before, Taylor used her free time between shows to write songs. But when she shared the first drafts of her new music with Scott Borchetta, the CEO of Big Machine, she started to have doubts. Even though Scott liked the album, Taylor realised that she wasn't convinced by the new tracks herself. She knew she could do something better.

Taylor decided the time had come to branch out and work with new collaborators. This brought her to the English singer-songwriter Ed Sheeran.

Taylor had loved Ed's debut album and wanted to work with him. Taylor and Ed had so much fun together. Once, when Ed was at Taylor's house, they were writing when Taylor suddenly blurted out, 'do you wanna see my trampoline? I just got one!'

Taylor hadn't even noticed she still had her guitar in her hand as she and Ed rushed out to the garden. While they were on the trampoline, Taylor played Ed an idea she'd had, which became the pre-chorus for 'Everything has Changed'!

Along with Ed, Taylor worked with a mix of new and old co-writers, but it was during the production process that things changed the most.

When Scott heard the songs that Taylor was working on, he suggested leaning towards a pop sound for the album. Though Taylor had dipped her toe into the pop genre before, she was still mostly considered a country artist. Changing her image within the industry could be risky, but Taylor had faith in herself that she could pull it off.

At Scott's suggestion she called Max Martin, a producer she had admired for years, and asked for his help in making her next album. He had worked with other legendary artists like Britney Spears, Beyoncé and Drake.

With Max on the project, Taylor created *Red*, an album with pop, country and even rock influences. Just like her previous albums, *Red* was about her experiences in relationships, but as Taylor had matured, so had her outlook on romance. *Red* was about the harder parts of relationships and adulthood. Alongside songs about the excitement and anxieties of getting older were themes of heartbreak, being single and finding power in friendships. This resulted in the era's defining songs: 'I Knew You Were Trouble', '22' and 'We Are Never Ever Getting Back Together', which became her first Billboard Hot Number One single!

Despite its pop focus, the album still earned nominations in the country categories at the Grammy Awards. It also earned

nods in broader categories, like Album of the Year, but sadly it didn't win.

Taylor decided to keep moving forward out of her comfort zone, and as she started working on her next album, she couldn't have imagined the impact it would have.

7

1989

Taylor was approaching ten years since her debut album and knew the time had come to redefine herself as an artist.

The first step was leaving Nashville. Taylor had lived there since she was fourteen years old, and she realised that to grow, she needed to follow a dream she'd had for a while: moving to New York. Though the move was significant for Taylor personally, it was also a dramatic change to her image as an artist. Moving away from the home of country music to the big city showed the world she was ready for exciting new things. It even inspired her song 'Welcome to New York', which was all about Taylor's excitement to explore her new home.

Critics had called *Red* a little disjointed and said that it wasn't totally clear what genre it was supposed to be.

So when it came to recording her new album, Taylor decided that it was going to be one hundred per cent pop. She asked Max Martin to help her make it, but she also wanted to work with a new producer called Jack Antonoff. Jack was a singer, and he and Taylor had worked well together before. For *1989*, they made two songs called 'I Wish You Would' and 'Out of the Woods'. This was the start of a special friendship between the two collaborators.

Just as her move to New York had inspired Taylor, so did music from the year she was born, which became the namesake of the album: *1989*. Taylor loved pop music from the late 1980s. She thought it was bold, energetic and vibrant. She wanted to capture that in her own album, which was her most adventurous and rebellious yet.

1989 was released in October 2014.

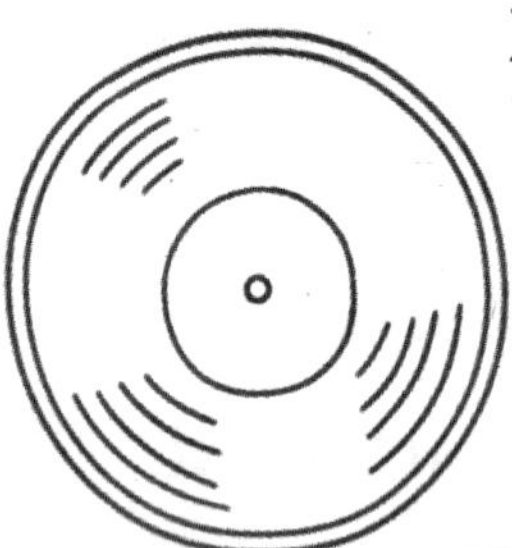

It peaked at number one on the album charts and had three number-one singles. The songs 'Shake It Off',

'Blank Space' and 'Bad Blood' became some of Taylor's most well-known and iconic songs. 'Style', rumoured to be about Taylor's fling with One Direction singer Harry Styles, became an instant fan favourite among Taylor's loyal followers, who had been given the nickname 'Swifties'.

Not only was the album a success in the charts, but it was praised by critics too and won Album of the Year at the Grammys! As she accepted the award, Taylor encouraged any young women watching to focus

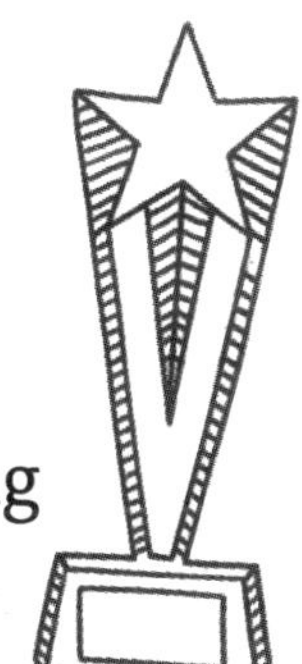

on their achievements. She also thanked everyone for giving her a moment to shine.

But while Taylor's career was reaching new heights, it felt like everyone was talking about her personal life. With her shift into the pop genre, Taylor discovered just how intense the public eye could be on pop stars. Once again, her relationships were in the spotlight.

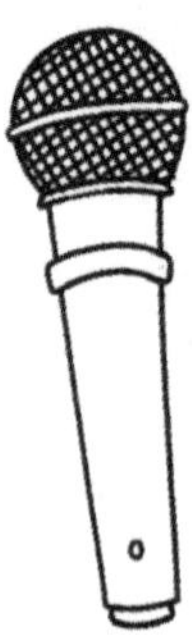

Her romance with Calvin Harris, a DJ from the UK, was followed closely by the media and fans alike. However, things didn't work out for Taylor and Calvin, and due to public pressure they decided to break up.

Her other two relationships during this era also came under scrutiny, especially her relationship with the actor Tom Hiddleston. A lot of people believed it was a 'showmance', meaning that they thought it was completely fake. Sadly, just like with Calvin, the weight of public pressure and gossip was too much for Taylor and Tom, and they broke up.

Another problem Taylor faced

during this era was a fight with music streaming services, who wanted to pay artists as little money as possible, despite the platforms being used by

millions of people. Taylor thought this was really unfair. She decided to take a stand, for herself and other artists.

Taylor had all her music removed from streaming services, refusing to let her work be taken advantage of. Only when her voice was heard and changes were introduced to support artists did she let her music return to streaming platforms.

Taylor had gone through a lot during this era. She had reached a new peak of fame, but also a new peak of criticism in the media. People were looking for any reason to say bad things about her, but none of it stopped Taylor, partly due to the close friends she had. And what better way to show off her Girl Squad than with an epic music video?

On the 17th of May 2015, the music video for 'Bad Blood' was released. It had a star-studded cast, including all of Taylor's close friends, such as the models Karlie Kloss and Gigi Hadid, singers Hayley Williams and Selena Gomez, the actress Zendaya and so many more. The song itself was believed to be about a feud Taylor had had with a former friend, the pop star Katy Perry. 'Bad Blood' was more than just Taylor making a statement following her argument with Katy, however. It proved that, despite being new to this version of fame and popularity and the challenges that came with it, she was more than capable of handling it. Although, the worst was still to come...

8

REPUTATION

After her most successful era yet, Taylor decided to take a break before working on her next album. The rest was well deserved following her *1989* world tour, but Taylor couldn't relax. How was she supposed to recreate the success she had achieved? The pressure was on, and things were about to get a lot harder.

Although Taylor thought things were good between her and Ye, in April 2016 she unexpectedly found herself in another dispute with him.

Ye had said something unkind about Taylor in one of his songs and stated that she'd given him permission for it. Taylor tried to tell the world that she had never given permission for Ye to say something so mean. But it was her word against his, and it made everyone turn on Taylor.

On social media, people commented on Taylor's posts with snake emojis, a symbol to show that they thought she was lying. Soon, it became impossible for Taylor to share anything online without being attacked by the public. So she took a step back and disappeared from the internet for a while.

Taylor was hurt. She felt like this incident had ruined her reputation. After winning over so many fans with *1989* and becoming one of the biggest pop stars in the world, she was now one of the most hated.

It was a scary time, but Taylor didn't let it stop her doing what she did best. Just like when she was a teenager in school, Taylor wrote songs about it all. People were waiting for Taylor's response, so the pressure was on to deliver something that would impress them. The result was her sixth album, *Reputation*, which would be her boldest piece of work yet.

Through her album, Taylor commented on the way people's view of her had shifted. The song 'Delicate' was about her fears that people wouldn't want to be friends with her any more, and 'Look What You Made Me Do' was about how she had been made into a villain by Ye. It was an album full of emotion – most of all anxiety. What if people didn't like her any more? What if they never did again?

Before the album's announcement she cleared her Instagram page of pictures, before posting a video of a snake. She wanted to reclaim the image that had been used to hurt her and call her a liar. The snake became the mascot for the Reputation era, showing her strength in the face of people who wanted to tear her down.

The music video for 'Look What You Made Me Do' was filled with messages for fans to find and work out. The video starts with a gravestone which reads: HERE LIES TAYLOR SWIFT'S REPUTATION. Later in the song, Taylor tells someone on the phone that the old Taylor is dead and gone. Taylor wanted to make sure everyone knew that she had changed and would not be defeated by what other people said or thought about her.

Despite her fears that no one would

listen to her music again, *Reputation* was a huge success. It was nominated for Best Pop Vocal Album at the 61st Annual Grammy Awards and was rated as one of her best albums yet by fans and critics alike. While her reputation was in pieces, Taylor showed her power to put it back together and craft something even stronger than what had come before.

To promote the album, Taylor travelled and performed in stadiums across the world. The shows opened with audio clips taken from Taylor's critics over the years, before launching into the album's opening song, '...Ready For It?' The tour was a huge success. It broke Taylor's own record as the highest-earning female-headlined tour, before smashing the record for the highest-earning tour in the USA ever!

By the end of the *Reputation* era, Taylor had grown and learnt from her past experiences. She was a pop icon, struggling with critics who wanted to see her fail, but finding new ways to prove them all wrong.

9

LOVER

As the *Reputation* stadium tour ended in November 2018, Taylor reflected on the era and how it had changed her as a person. She was now thirteen years into her career – her lucky number – and had made a name for herself as a global star.

When Taylor had first signed

her contract with Big Machine as a teenager, she could only have dreamt of how big she would become. She had agreed to make and promote six albums for them. She had also agreed that she wouldn't own any of her master recordings – something she later regretted. Master recordings are the original recordings of songs, and whoever owns them makes most of the money from sales and streaming.

With the end of the *Reputation* era, Taylor had completed her contract with Big Machine and was free to move elsewhere.

Republic Records, her new record label, agreed to let her keep the master recordings of all her future work, and the songs on her new album, *Lover*, would be the first of those masters.

During the recording of *Reputation*, Taylor had met the British actor Joe Alwyn, and the two started a relationship. This romance had inspired a few songs on *Reputation* that talked about discovering a new love. But *Lover* was heavily inspired by her time with Joe. Where her other albums had talked about the spark of new love, the new album was about being in a long-term relationship.

The first single from the album was 'ME!', released in April 2019. The music video opened with a black and white snake bursting into pastel-coloured butterflies, declaring the end of the *Reputation* era.

With this big shift, Taylor was also showing her audience that she had moved on from her past and was focused on the present.

The launch of this new era was a great time for Taylor. She was singing about someone she loved, and her

Swifties had remained loyal throughout the hardest moments of her career so far.

But just as things had started to look up for Taylor, she got some difficult news.

When Taylor was planning her next tour, she found out her mother was really sick. Taylor was so upset. Her mother was her best friend. Taylor didn't want to be away from her for too long, so she scheduled her worldwide Lover Fest tour to be shorter than her previous ones.

Even more bad news followed.

In 2020, a horrible disease called COVID-19 spread across the world. Lots of countries went into lockdown, with people told to stay in their homes. Taylor had to cancel all her performances – including her tour.

Taylor had even been set to perform at the 2020 Glastonbury Festival in the UK. Playing at Glastonbury is a big deal for artists. Only really big names are invited to take to the stage. And Taylor had not just been asked to perform – she'd been asked to headline! This meant she would be one of the main performers at the festival. Taylor was so gutted when the festival was cancelled. 'It's so sad,' she said, 'but I know it's the right decision.' Taylor's top priority was making sure everyone was safe, but she hoped to be back performing for her fans again soon.

10

TAYLOR'S VERSION

Amid all these challenges, the issue of her master records began to cause problems for Taylor. Scott Borchetta decided to sell Big Machine to Scooter Braun, a music producer who had helped Justin Bieber become famous.

When Scooter bought Big Machine, he also got the master records of all of

Taylor's songs, meaning she wouldn't make any more money from them. This was a huge problem for Taylor and really upset her. There was very little she could do about it, but that didn't mean she didn't have a plan.

With the news of the sale of Big Machine, everyone was waiting for Taylor's reaction. After raising her voice during the *Reputation* era, people expected her to do something, though it was hard to predict *what*... That was until another singer, Kelly Clarkson, offered Taylor some really important advice.

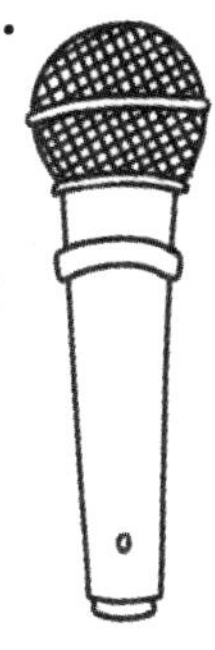

She suggested that Taylor should re-record all of her old songs and re-release them.

Taylor did exactly that. Her old contract with Big Machine said she didn't own the master records, but there were no rules about re-recording the original songs to create *new* masters.

Taylor got straight to work on her earlier albums. The first re-recorded album to be released was *Fearless (Taylor's Version)*, which came out in 2021. While Taylor had done just what Kelly suggested, she made a few changes to the album too. The album had a new cover and additional tracks. These new songs were called 'Vault Tracks' and were songs that Taylor had written for the original album that were never released. *Fearless (Taylor's Version)* was a huge success, going to number one on the Billboard charts. The new version of 'Love Story' also went to number one.

The next re-recorded album she released, later in 2021, was *Red (Taylor's Version)*. It was supported by the single 'All Too Well (10 Minute Version)' which became the longest song in history to hit the Billboard charts.

The success of both re-recorded albums proved that fans supported Taylor on this new journey, and it encouraged her to keep going.

In 2023, she re-recorded and released *Speak Now (Taylor's Version)* and that same year she also released *1989 (Taylor's Version)* and the single 'Is It Over Now?'

She had just two more albums to re-record: *Taylor Swift* and *Reputation*. She was ready to reclaim them both.

11

FOLKLORE AND EVERMORE

Before she had started work on the re-recorded albums, Taylor had a couple of surprises for her fans. Due to COVID-19 and the lockdowns that happened throughout 2020, Taylor had something she'd rarely had before: free time at home! With her

Lover Fest tour postponed and later cancelled, she was free to work on something new. The result was two new albums: *Folklore* and *Evermore*.

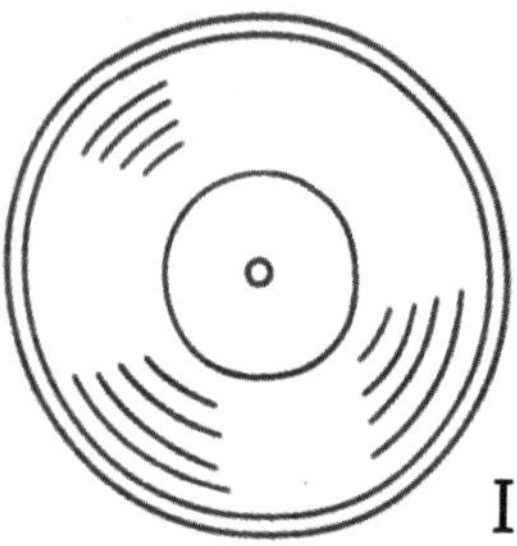

After *Lover*'s more personal songwriting, Taylor decided it was time to change her process. Instead of writing about her life, she wanted to write about other people's lives.

One of these people was Rebekah Harkness, who had lived in Taylor's home, 'Holiday House' on Rhode Island, long before her. The song

'The Last Great American Dynasty' was all about Rebekah's life as an outcast in an elite society, a situation that fans were sure Taylor had related to during her early years on the pop music scene.

She also invented new characters for the album, such as lovers James and Betty from the song 'Betty'.

This was refreshing for Taylor, but so was the production team she chose to work with. The only person returning from her last few albums was record producer Jack Antonoff.

For *Folklore* she teamed up with Aaron Dessner and Justin Vernon. Taylor's boyfriend Joe Alwyn also contributed to the album. To keep his role in the writing process a secret, he was credited using the false name William Bowery.

The album was mostly produced virtually, with the team sending vocals and lyrics to one another without meeting in person. It was totally different to any other album Taylor had put out before, but it was still a huge success,

winning Taylor her third Album of the Year at the Grammys!

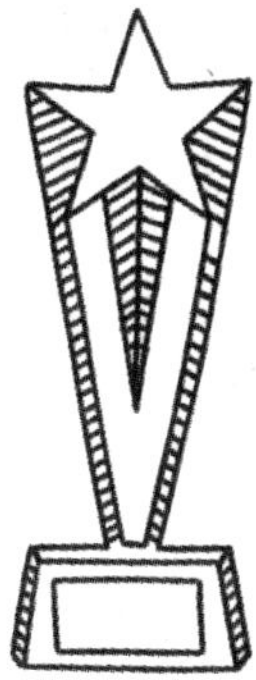

Part of what made *Folklore* so special was the suddenness of its arrival. Unlike previous albums when Taylor had teased them ahead of time and released singles, *Folklore* came out of nowhere, releasing the same day it was announced. She didn't even tell Republic Records about the album until the day it was released! She had been so proud of it that she decided to share it with the world the second it was ready.

And just as people thought the surprises were done, Taylor announced *Folklore*'s sister album, *Evermore*, six months later. They were known as sister albums because they shared the same sound and themes.

Repeating what she had done with *Folklore*, Taylor announced *Evermore* in an Instagram post just

hours before it was released. But unlike *Folklore*, *Evermore* was a return to more personal songwriting and focused on Taylor's emotions rather than fictional or historical people. Once again, she worked with Jack, Aaron, Justin and Joe, but also with Alana, Danielle and Este Haim, three sisters who were members of the band Haim.

Like *Folklore*, *Evermore* was immediately successful. Fans and critics loved it, and it was nominated for Album of the Year at the Grammys, just one year after Taylor had won for *Folklore*!

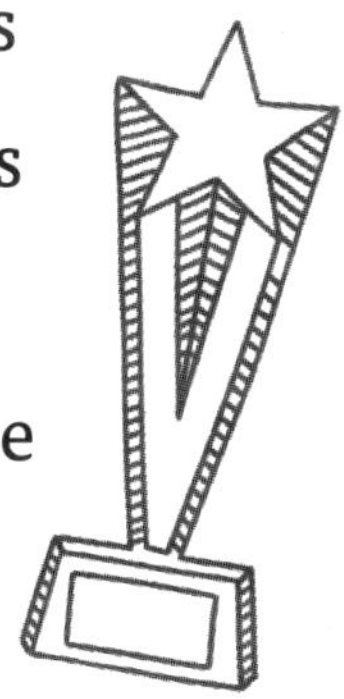

After a rocky few years, Taylor was finally proving to the world what she already knew about herself: she had the ability to adapt and keep surprising her audience.

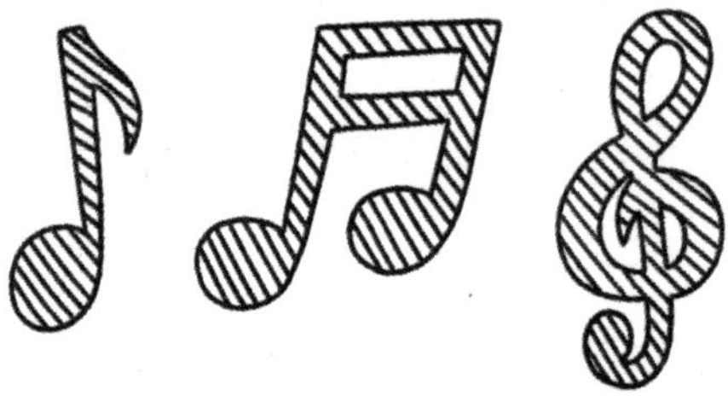

12

MIDNIGHTS

Two years after the release of *Evermore*, Taylor was back with her tenth studio album, *Midnights*. After the more acoustic sound of her previous two albums, Taylor returned to the synth-pop sound that she loved. Once again, Taylor wrote this album over a twelve-month period, with Jack Antonoff by her side. This time, no singles were released prior to the album dropping. Taylor didn't even give any interviews beforehand. All fans knew were the song titles, which were revealed one by one in the run up to the launch.

Midnights was released at midnight on the 21st of October 2022. Just three hours later, Taylor followed it up with *Midnights (3am Edition)*, which featured seven bonus tracks. And it wasn't the only deluxe version of the album. In May 2023, *Midnights (The Til Dawn Edition)* was released, featuring three more bonus tracks.

On the same day that *Midnights* was first released, the music video for the lead single 'Anti-Hero' also came out. It became an instant hit, entering the Billboard Hot 100 chart at number one and getting 17 million first-day streams on Spotify – the highest number of first-day streams in the platform's history!

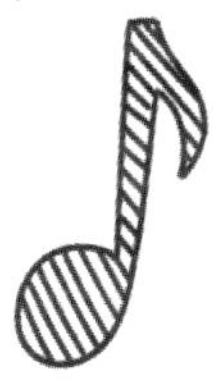

The song resonated with fans because of its honest yet catchy lyrics, as Taylor vulnerably criticises herself. Taylor said the song was one of her favourites she had ever written, as it allowed her to explore her own insecurities.

Midnights saw Taylor return

once again to writing songs about her own life and feelings, and she attributed each track on the album to one of 'thirteen sleepless nights' she'd had throughout her life.

'Karma' touched upon Taylor's belief that good deeds attract good things, and that the people who have wronged her will have bad karma. Meanwhile, 'Mastermind' explored Taylor's desire to carefully plan her life and relationships.

On the 24th of February 2024, as Taylor accepted her Grammy for Best Pop Vocal Album for *Midnights*, she announced: 'I want to say thank you to the fans by telling you a secret that I've been keeping from you for the last two years, which is that my brand-new album comes out on April 19th. It's called *The Tortured Poets Department*.'

Taylor also went on to win her fourth Album of the Year award later in the evening!

13

THE TORTURED POETS DEPARTMENT

Even though she was performing tirelessly on tour in the USA in 2023, Taylor had been working hard on her new album behind the scenes. She'd wasted no time and started writing a new album as soon as she'd submitted *Midnights* to her record

label for release.

The Tortured Poets Department (TTPD) was released on the 19th of April 2024. It was clear to fans that the lively electropop vibe of *Midnights* wasn't sticking around. *TTPD* brought a more downbeat and folk-inspired sound, though Taylor's country roots could still be heard in songs like 'But Daddy I Love Him'. The album also featured collaborations with Post Malone and Florence + The Machine.

Being such a prolific songwriter, Taylor packed *TTPD* with tracks and it was her longest album to date. The deluxe edition, called *The Anthology* and released two hours after the main album, has thirty-one tracks. Taylor became the first artist to claim all top fourteen positions on the Billboard Hot 100! The lead single of the album, 'Fortnight', held the number one spot.

With a more gothic, gloomy feel to the album art, *TTPD* was a lot more experimental than Taylor's previous albums, which caused a bit of a rift among fans

when it was released. The album was even more personal than her previous work, and it was true to its title with detailed, poetic lyrics. Listeners heard songs about pining over forbidden love, lost dreams and Taylor's desires to escape the public eye. But there were still plenty of pop tunes to be heard on *TTPD*, such as 'My Boy Only Breaks His Favourite Toys' and 'I Can Do It With a Broken Heart'.

The run-up to the album's release had been an eventful time

in the Taylor Swift fandom. It had

become clear that Taylor was no longer in a relationship with Joe Alwyn after she was seen with Matty Healy, the lead singer of The 1975, during May and June 2023.

Between Matty making an appearance on stage during Taylor's tour and the pair mouthing secret messages to each other on stage, the fandom was set alight with

opinions about this intense but short-lived romance.

As a result, some songs on the album caused a frenzy among Swifties as they tried to figure out who the songs were about. Where they had expected the songs to be about Joe Alwyn, fans suspected most were really about Matty Healy.

But earlier heartbreak was ultimately overshadowed by Taylor's blossoming relationship with American footballer Travis Kelce. The two confirmed their relationship in October 2023 after Taylor was spotted at one of Travis's games.

Two of the few happy songs on *TTPD* were likely about Taylor's relationship with Travis: 'The Alchemy' and 'So High School'. Both songs are romantic and upbeat, matching how Taylor felt about her relationship.

Despite the album being deeply personal, Taylor still included some songs inspired by fiction, like 'Cassandra', which is based on the Greek myth about a woman who could see the future but was cursed to never be listened to.

The Tortured Poets Department was yet another record-breaking album for Taylor, even before it was released. *TTPD* became the most pre-saved album of all time on Spotify! The album went on to reach 313 million first-day streams on the platform and become the most streamed album in a single day, breaking the all-time record previously held by *Midnights*.

It also meant an addition to the highest-earning tour of all time: The Eras Tour.

14

THE ERAS TOUR

On the evening of the 17th of March 2023, during the promotion of *Midnights*, Taylor was about to take to the stage for the first performance of The Eras Tour. It was her first major tour in over five years and a showcase of her entire music career. There was a section for every album Taylor had released, with a part added for *The Tortured Poets Department* which dropped while Taylor was on the road.

The audience was buzzing with anticipation, excited to follow Taylor as she guided them through the heartbreak of *Fearless*, the freedom of *1989*, the emotional depth of *Red*, and the boldness of *Midnights*. And, of course, the magic of *Lover*, *Folklore* and *Evermore*.

As the show began, Taylor's dancers manoeuvred large peachy fabric fans around the stage, pulling them together to hide Taylor ready for her big entrance. In the blink of an eye, the fans were drawn back and

Taylor was revealed, glittering in a bejewelled pink and blue bodysuit. She immediately launched into 'Miss Americana & the Heartbreak Prince' – and just like that, The Eras Tour had begun!

The tour took fans – and Taylor – on an emotional journey. In the early shows, Swifties noticed Taylor tearing up while singing 'Lover', 'tolerate it' and 'champagne problems'. It later came out that she was breaking up with Joe Alwyn at the time, explaining why the songs had affected her so much. In *The Tortured Poets Department*, Taylor captured what she had been going through in 'I Can Do It With a Broken Heart', a song about putting on a show while secretly hurting inside. As the tour went on, however, fans began to see Taylor perform with more and more joy. She was beginning to feel much happier, and her new love with Travis was blossoming behind the scenes.

With a set list of around forty-six songs, performed over three and a half hours, the Eras Tour was groundbreaking. The first show smashed the record for the most-attended concert by a female artist at the time! Over the course of the tour, Taylor performed almost her entire discography, with only six songs missing from her set list. The Swifties danced so much that some of the concerts registered on the Richter scale, which is a scale used to measure earthquakes!

Though it mostly ran smoothly and

broke seven stadium records, fans affectionately dubbed the tour The Errors Tour. From wardrobe malfunctions to sets not moving like they were supposed to, mishaps were rife. Taylor even swallowed two bugs mid-performance over the course of the tour! A compilation of these funny moments were shown in the end credits of *Taylor Swift: The Eras Tour*, which was played in cinemas to make sure all fans got to experience the magic. It went on to be the highest-grossing concert film of all time.

On the final night of the tour, Taylor said, 'I want to thank every single one of you for being a part of the most thrilling chapter of my life so far.' It was the end of an era, but there were so many more to come.

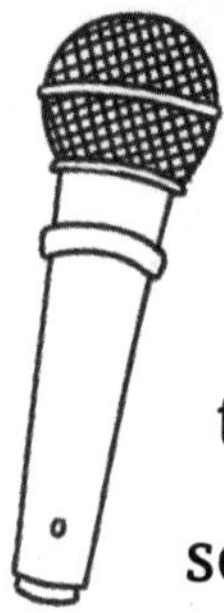

In August 2025, Taylor announced that she would be dropping yet another new album: *The Life of a Showgirl*. Inspired by her time touring over the last couple of years, Taylor wanted to create an upbeat album covering the glitz and glamour of life on the stage – and of being in love.

Just after she announced the album to the world, Travis surprised Taylor with a romantic gesture. Surrounded by hundreds of pink and white roses, he got down on one knee and asked her to marry him. Taylor was living out her very own love story!

From being a little girl who dreamt of being a country singer to one of the biggest stars in the world, Taylor continues to inspire other young people to follow their dreams and never say never. She believes that you can never succeed if you let fear of failure or judgement hold you back.

'Fearless doesn't necessarily mean that you don't have any fears,' she explained when discussing the title of her second album. 'Sometimes being fearless means having fears but jumping anyway.'

For Taylor, the most important thing is to keep creating art. Through her songs, she tells the world about her innermost feelings and desires, and it helps her to manage her emotions. No matter what anyone says, Taylor is determined to keep writing and use her music to unite fans and express herself.